LINDA TOUBY

BEVERLY HILLS, CALIFORNIA

2007

LINDA TOUBY

BEVERLY HILLS, CALIFORNIA
2007

title page: *Homage to Giotto, #101, oil and wax on linen, 84" x 72"*

cover detail: *Homage to Giotto, #32, oil and wax on linen, 42" x 50", pg. 49*

ESSAY: Janet Kardon; Independent Curator, Former Director American Craft Museum, New York, NY
Former Director Institute of Contemporary Art, University of Pennsylvania

PROJECT COORDINATOR, EDITOR: Judy Lambert

DESIGN: MJ Design, San Francisco, CA

PHOTOGRAPHY: Ryan Fernandez, New York, NY

PUBLISHED IN THE UNITED STATES BY YARGER ARTS, INC.

YEAR: 2007

ISBN: 1-930157-14-2

CATALOGUE EDITION SIZE: 1,100

PRINTING: South Korea

The history of art is memorialized by the creation and exploration of distinguished styles by select artists. Linda Touby is one such artist and it is with pride that we record within these pages for posterity a remarkable collection of paintings created especially for this important exhibition. This publication honors the long, rich relationship between Timothy Yarger Fine Art and Linda Touby while also illustrating the spectacular results of Touby's rigorous artistic journey.

In addition, we offer our great appreciation to Janet Kardon for her eloquent essay on Touby's work. Kardon brings her extensive museum experience and personal involvement with artists to bear on this poignant, articulate, and informative introduction.

Please join us in celebrating this milestone in the career of Linda Touby.

Enjoy!

TIMOTHY YARGER
FINE ART
BEVERLY HILLS • BANGKOK

Homage to Giotto #8, oil and wax on linen, 56" x 56"

Homage to Giotto #69, oil and wax on linen, 40" x 60"

Linda Touby in studio, 2006

As a painter in the early 21st century, committed to abstraction, how do you paint in an innovative style without echoing the overpowering statements of the abstract expressionists or color field artists? Linda Touby has studied the painting techniques of masters of different eras as divergent as Richard Pousette Dart, Hans Hofmann, Cimabue, and Giotto. By creating paintings that reflect these lessons and yet engage present issues, her contribution is significant.

Each painting emerges from the process of layering one color on another on another, an ongoing contest in which the finished painting is not derived from preliminary sketches, but from the actual process that is dependent upon the manipulation of color passages. The canvas is often divided by a horizontal, surrounded above and below by areas that could be sky and earth, resulting in the format of a landscape study. Like Monet's haystacks, each of which changed as the sun moved, Touby's works depict a

LINDA TOUBY

private territory with different views of nature dispensed through the deployment of varying palettes and surfaces. Akin to Monet's recording of the movement of the sun in each new canvas, Touby presents groups of works that navigate imaginary universes. Each canvas records a unique vision of a place that is defined by layers of color, permeated by glimpses of light and made almost palpable through the texture of paint.

Changes in scale are managed effortlessly. Her vision is equally dispersed in macrocosmic or microcosmic proportions. Brushstrokes are malleable and easily adjust in the process of painting to the scale of the canvas.

Different works reveal a variety of techniques and sources. Touby works directly on about four paintings at a time, constantly revising each surface through innovative and intuitive actions. She most often works in oils with a wax medium, a recipe taken from Rembrandt. There is often evidence in the finished paintings of the steps that were taken to produce it. Glazes intervene with oil passages. Adhesive tape is used to remove and add elements. Oil sticks, or crayons are applied to thin layers of dried paint. Pure color powder in a wax medium spreads easily as a final layer, bringing clear vivid colors and light to the paintings. A foundation of red may be barely visible yet can be perceived through close examination of the crevices of thickly painted layers. In one painting, Homage to Giotto # 8, based on exposure to an exotic African animal in a zoo, ephemeral traces of stripes and fur appear in the paint. The markings of wild animals- snakes, zebras, giraffes- brings another textural element into the painting.

Homage to Giotto #8, pg. 5

The recent series, Homage to Giotto, begun in 2002, reflects her studies of that master. Painterly surfaces are broken into rectangular subdivisions. Each canvas is ruled by the prominence of a few selected colors, each assigned to an isolated segment of the canvas. These horizontal films of color are not unlike Rothko's color passages. But Touby's surfaces are much more active, revealing much more evidence of individual brush strokes. Color is an accumulation of these markings, blended directly onto the canvas itself.

Homage to Giotto #34 contains five horizontal areas. Red is the prominent color in two of the passages, and three areas are blue and a mottled gray. The blue trespasses in to red areas and gray areas, and one slender ribbon at the base of the canvas acts to accentuate the edge. As in other works, the wider band at mid-canvas acts as a horizon line. While eschewing a frame that is a separate element, the proportions of a thin linear painted edge on the right and left sides suggest a frame within a frame.

Homage to Giotto #34, pg. 45

The color palette of Homage to Giotto #73 is dominated by blues, grays and greens. The canvas is again divided in half by a horizontal stripe of brilliant blue, and each vertical edge is accentuated by a slim painted line. The upper portion of the work contains dark murky passages; the lower half is filled with light permeated cloud-like forms. It is surprising that the darker area of the top section of the painting can co-exist with the lower, much lighter half. As in many of the works the surface is mottled, active, and energized by brushstrokes that read with a freshness and vitality.

Homage to Giotto #73, pg. 38

Colors in a turmoil and brush strokes in frenzy characterize the active painterly surface of the most complex work in the series, Homage to Giotto #69. Each of the three rectangular areas is governed by its own maelstrom of paint application. The surface resounds with the energy of a deKooning passage but the mix of colors and infinite spatial dynamics are characteristic of Touby's painting. Receding blues are brought forward by dashes of yellows; aggressive reds are cooled by black intervals. Deep spatial interludes are held in place by contrasting hues. Wax mixed with pigment, added to oil layers conveys unlimited depth, while brighter layers adhere to the surface.

Homage to Giotto #69, pg. 6

Touby also works in a more diminutive scale. Homage to Giotto #84 is 24 inches square, and is divided into primary color segments, progressing from a yellow top band to horizontal passages of first red and then blue. Without suggestion of a horizon line, and with a primary palette, the painting lacks an easy reference to nature. This is not to say that a sense of space is absent. Instead there is an infinite dialogue between surface and color that seems to enable the pigment to float in front of the canvas, while like a faceted jewel; the depth of the painting is an infinite dimension.

Touby's paintings should be perceived in the historic continuum of abstract painting. (She actually studied with Richard Poisette Dart.) Her work reflects the groundbreaking innovations of some of the original abstract expressionists, such as Rothko or deKooning, as well as the lessons of a few of their successors as illustrated by Joan Mitchell or the German Neo-Expressionists.

Ultimately, her work is devoted to an ongoing investigation into color and multiple means of paint manipulation. Each painting transcends its dimensions as it reaches for the infinite. The body of work taken in concert proclaims the synergy of the medium and the message.

– Janet Kardon
Independent Curator
Former Director American Craft Museum, New York, NY
Former Director Institute of Contemporary Art, University of Pennsylvania

Homage to Giotto #84, pg. 48

Homage to Giotto, #1, oil and wax on masonite, 8" x 10"

Homage to Giotto, #2, oil and wax on masonite, 8" x 10"

Homage to Giotto, #72, oil and wax on linen, 40" x 60"

Homage to Giotto, #90, oil and wax on linen, 18" x 18"

Homage to Giotto, #75, oil and wax on linen, 46" x 46"

Homage to Giotto, #76, oil and wax on linen, 42" x 42"

Homage to Giotto, #74, oil and wax on linen, 50" x 60"

Homage to Giotto, #17, oil and wax on linen, 24" x 24"

Homage to Giotto, #80, oil and wax on linen, 30" x 40"

Homage to Giotto, #86, oil and wax on linen, 20" x 20"

Homage to Giotto, #67, oil and wax on linen, 52" x 52"

Homage to Giotto, #14, oil and wax on linen, 36" x 36"

Homage to Giotto, #65, oil and wax on linen, 56" x 56"

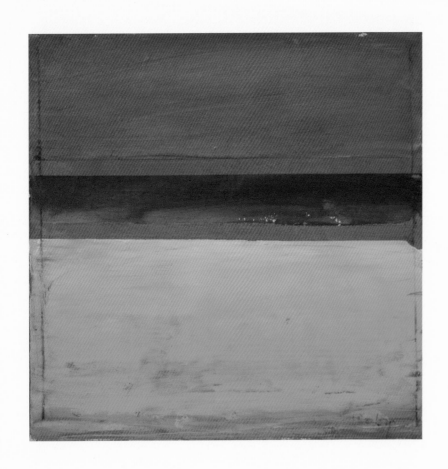

Homage to Giotto, #88, oil and wax on linen, 20"x 20"

Homage to Giotto, #7, oil and wax on linen, 56" x 56"

Homage to Giotto, #78, oil and wax on linen, 36" x 36"

Homage to Giotto, #31, oil and wax on linen, 38" x 50"

Homage to Giotto, #89, oil and wax on linen, 20" x 20"

Homage to Giotto, #10, oil and wax on linen, 42" x 50"

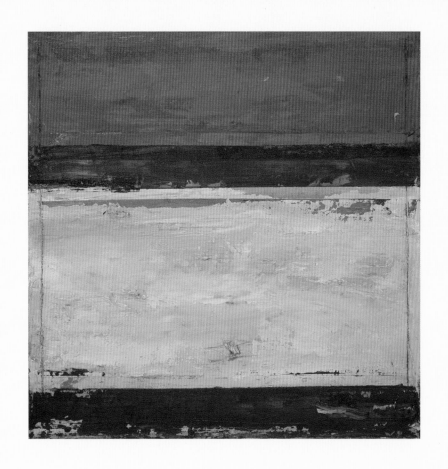

Homage to Giotto, #83, oil and wax on linen, 24" x 24"

Homage to Giotto, #81, oil and wax on linen, 30" x 34"

Homage to Giotto, #73, oil and wax on linen, 44" x 60"

Homage to Giotto, #33, oil and wax on linen, 42" x 50"

Homage to Giotto, #82, oil and wax on linen, 28" x 38"

Homage to Giotto, #77, oil and wax on linen, 38" x 36"

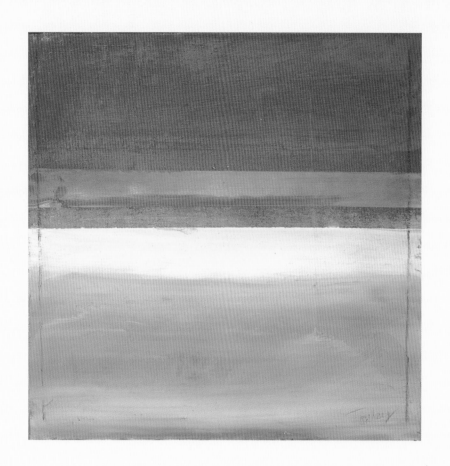

Homage to Giotto, #91, oil and wax on linen, 18" x 18"

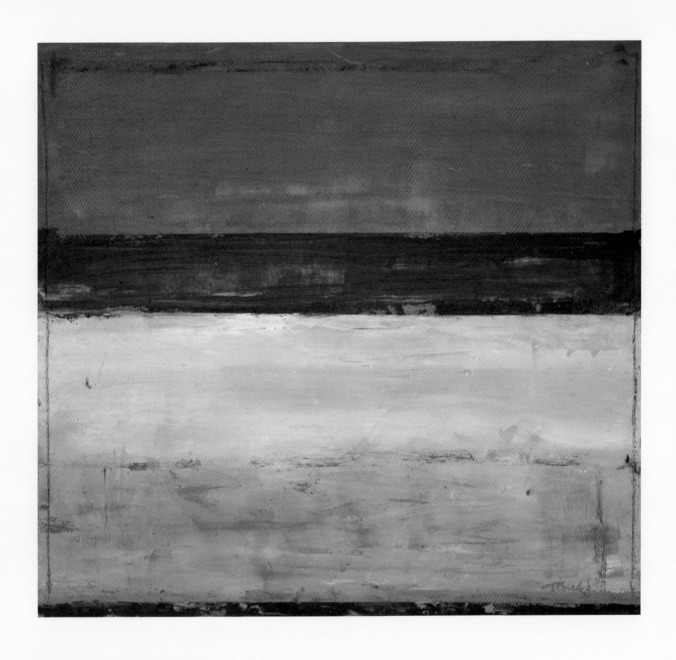

Homage to Giotto, #11, oil and wax on linen, 46" x 50"

Homage to Giotto, #13, oil and wax on linen, 42" x 42"

Homage to Giotto, #34, oil and wax on linen, 46" x 50"

Homage to Giotto, #85, oil and wax on linen, 24" x 24"

Homage to Giotto, #28, oil and wax on linen, 58" x 68"

Homage to Giotto, #84, oil and wax on linen, 24" x 24"

Homage to Giotto, #32, oil and wax on linen, 42" x 50"

Homage to Giotto, #87, oil and wax on linen, 20" x 20"

Homage to Giotto, #70, oil and wax on linen, 40" x 60"

Homage to Giotto, #60, oil and wax on linen, 56" x 56"

Homage to Giotto, #61, oil and wax on linen, 56" x 56"

Sketch For Sand, oil and wax on paper, 40" x 28"

Ulyseses' Journey, #X , oil and wax on paper, 30" x 22"

Ulyseses' Journey, #CX, oil and wax on paper, 22" x 30"

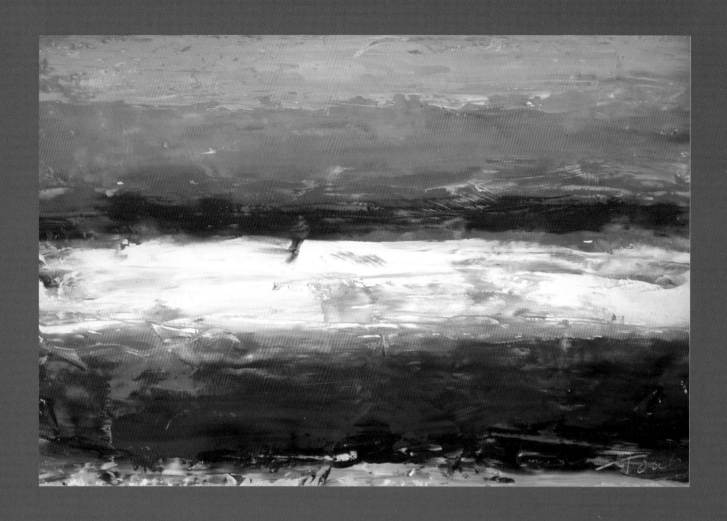

Sketch, Homage to Giotto, #5, oil and wax on paper, 26" x 40"

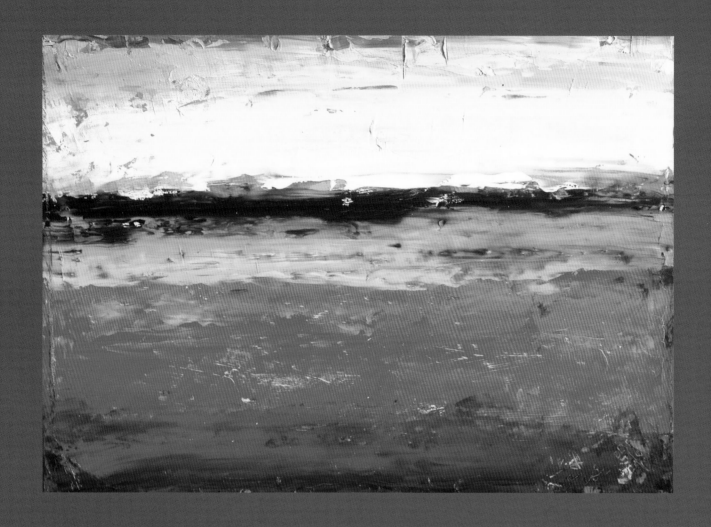

Sketch, Homage to Giotto, #4, oil and wax on paper, 28" x 39"

Sketch, Homage to Giotto, #1 oil and wax on paper, 28" x 40"

Sketch, Homage to Giotto, #2, oil and wax on paper, 26" x 40"

Sketch, Homage to Giotto, #3, oil and wax on paper, 26" x 40"

BIOGRAPHY

EDUCATION

Pratt Institute, Brooklyn, NY
Art Students' League, New York, NY
National Academy of Art, New York, NY

SELECTED BIBLIOGRAPHY

2007 Timothy Yarger Fine Art catalog, text by Janet Kardon

2005 United States Embassy Algiers catalog, Robert Soppelsa,
Curator

2004 Art in Embassy Program, 40th anniversary catalog, text by
Andrew Solomon

United States Embassy, Tunis, Tunisia, catalog text by Imtiaz
Hafiz, curator Virginia Shore

2000 Provincetown Arts, "Abstract Expression without the Angst:
Linda Touby's Instructive Popularity" by Eleanor Kennelly

"Linda Touby Freedom, Harmony and Painting", catalog text
by Susan Inniss

1999 Und, Das Munchener Kunstjournal, No. 8 "Amerikanische
Kunstler in Munchen" by Matthias Schubler

1998 Washington Post, "Grand Gestures in Painting", by Ferdinand
Protzman

1997 "The Critical State of Visual Art in New York", by J. Bowler Bell
The Miami Herald, "Language of Paint Colors, Two Shows" by
Elisa Turner

Linda Touby's "Heroic Quest for the Grand Gesture", catalog text
by Ed McCormack

1996 Mallorca Post, "Spiel Mit Licht Udn Farben"
Dia Del Mundo, "Linda Touby, Expone en Blanvar Estudio"
La Vox de Baleares, "Linda Touby"
Ultima Hora, "La Pintora, Americana, Linda Touby Expone en
Palma su Expresionismo Constructivista"
Correo Del Arte, "Ritmo Y Color En La OBra De Linda Touby"

1995 Correo Del Arte, "Linda Touby at Goya Art Gallery"

1993 New York Times, "In Your Own Backyard, Some Mysterious
Goings On" by Vivien Raynor

Engadiner Post, "Three American Artists Erstmal Inder Schweiz"

1992 Down Town Express, "Linda Touby" by Debra Webber,
Alex Gallery, "Seven Artists", catalog text by Eleanor Kennelly,

1991 "The Cherry Blossom Series", catalog text by Anastasia Bride
Washington Post, "Touby at Alex" by Janet Wilson

ONE PERSON EXHIBITIONS

2007 **Timothy Yarger Fine Art**, Beverly Hills, CA
2006 **United States Embassy**, Kuwait City, Kuwait
Bill Hodges Gallery, New York, NY
Madelyn Jordan Fine Art, New York, NY
2005 **Timothy Yarger Fine Art**, Beverly Hills, CA
Alex Gallery, Washington, D.C.
Rice/Polak Gallery, Provincetown, MA

2004 **Alex Gallery**, Washington, D.C.
2003 **Landor Fine Arts**, Newark, NJ
Alex Gallery, Washington, D.C
2002 **Timothy Yarger Galleries**, Santa Monica, CA
2001 **Alex Gallery**, Washington, D.C.
Galerie Rieder, Munchen, Germany
2000 **Bill Hodges Gallery**, New York, NY
Alex Gallery, Washington, D.C.
1998 **Alex Gallery**, Washington, D.C.
1997 **Artspace/Virginia Miller Galleries**, Coral Gables, FL
Bill Hodges Gallery, New York, NY
Casa De Agua, Palencia, Spain
1996 **Blanvar Estudio Galeria De Arte**, Palma De Mallorca, Spain
Galleria de Arte Novart Monte, Esquinza, Spain
1995 **Alex Gallery**, Washington, D.C
La Mama La Galleria, New York, NY
1993 **Tribeca Gallery**, New York, NY

SELECTED MUSEUM EXHIBTIONS

2005 **Provincetown Art Association and Museum**, Provincetown, MA
2004 **Vero Beach Museum of Art**, Vero Beach, FL
2003 **Provincetown Art Association and Museum**, Provincetown, MA
1999 **Museum Fur Knonkrete Kunst Ingolstadt**, Munchen, Germany
Amerika Haus Karolenstrasse, Munchen, Germany
1998 **Provincetown Art Association and Museum**, Provincetown, MA
1997 **Sa Nostra**, Palma De Mallorca, Spain
1995 **Albright-Knox Gallery**, Buffalo, New York
1993 **The Gallerie Roseg**, Moritz, Switzerland
Castle Gallery College of New Rochelle, New Rochelle, NY
Curated by Lucinda Gideon Ph.D., Director of Neuberger
Museum of Art
1990 **Museum of Realism and Atheism**, Lvov, Ukraine

SELECTED PUBLIC COLLECTIONS

General Motors Corporation, USA
Phillips Corporation, USA
American Embassy, Ambassador Richard LeBaron,
Kuwait City, Kuwait
American Embassy, Ambassador John Danilovich,
San Jose, Costa Rica
American Embassy, American Ambassador Richard Erdman,
Algiers
American Embassy, American Ambassador Rust Deming,
Tunis, Tunisia
American Embassy, American Ambassador William Melam,
Islamabad, Pakistan
Professional Indemnity Agency, Inc., USA Headquarters,
New York, NY
Bertholon-Rowland Corporation, New York, NY
United States State Department, Washington, D.C.

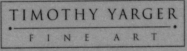

329 North Beverly Drive
Beverly Hills
California 90210

TEL 310.278.4400
FAX 310.278.6771
www.yargerfineart.com

Suite 11, Ground Floor
The Promenade Decor
2/4 Wireless Road
Bangkok 10330

TEL 02.655.0882

TIMOTHY YARGER

FINE ART

BEVERLY HILLS • BANGKOK

329 North Beverly Drive
Beverly Hills
California 90210

TEL 310.278.4400
FAX 310.278.6771
www.yargerfineart.com

Suite 11, Ground Floor
The Promenade Decor
2/4 Wireless Road
Bangkok 10330

TEL 02.655.0882